we / sun people /

mypeople

Khaliah D. Pitts

Black Minds Publishing is a national publications platform centered around the personal and professional growth of artists and creatives of the Black diaspora. At Black Minds Publishing we aim to give more visibility to raw artistic works, both literary and visual, that center on the healing process of the Black mind, body and spirit. We aren't concerned with the rigid expectations of academia or the "supposed to's" of artistic gatekeepers and instead choose to prioritize genuine works that have meaningful impact for its readers.

Names: Khaliah D. Pitts

Title: we / sun people / mypeople

Description: Philadelphia, PA: Black Minds Publishing [2023]

Identifiers: 978-1-7375490-8-6

BLACK MINDS PUBLISHING

Table of Contents

the Nigga face

there is an allure to the nigga face— like god blew gold dust across
black-fertile earth it is a map then, brimming with creasings and ley lines,
tropics and the dance of tides the nigga face is a here now / now here /
nowhere / been there / been every-fuckin-where

she, of big nose, big lips, scarab eyes and—
etched again and again in clay, in stone, in earth, in body, by hands, by
nonbelievers, by— the nigga face is a here now / now here / nowhere /
been there / been every-fuckin-where

she, of "hold this" shelf-shoulders, "keep this safe" breasts, and—
called hottentot and now thot— slandered by babies, by lovers, by self, by
slurs, by prayer, by— there is an allure to the nigga face— like god blew
gold dust across black-fertile earth

she, of art, of monument, of Madonna, of adam and—
sculpted in dung, in soil, in water, in ocean waves, in sand, by hungry
eyes, by jealous lies, by— the nigga face is a here now / now here / no-
where / been there / been every-fuckin-where

she. she. she. she. of nigga face, of Black faith, of woman-place, and—
drank in like milk that come by tit, that come by bless, that come by, come
by, come by— there is an allure to the nigga face— like god blew gold dust
across black-fertile earth cause the nigga face is a here now / now here /
nowhere / been there / been every-fuckin-where.

Grandmother Rice // basic instructions before leaving the earth

it is dark / in the beginning
always, always
folded into neat corn rows
plump, luscious, kinked like bramble, corn rows
i was so close to an earth

it was hot and i was like the sun

//

it is dark in the
beginning always, always
snatched from cradle, and

planted, urgently
among rows— rows and rows and—
when would we see the sun

again? when, where would
we be Sun? the earth cried and
broke and bleed perhaps

death was preferable
to this. the sea maybe pre—
ferable to this. don't

niggas need water
too?

that was the beginning

//

the rice used to sing in the voices

of shadowy black specters

massa don't know that language, son
dis sun language, here

the niggas sang sun language back
sweet voices that baptize the blood

it is a sun language we speak
and massa can't hear us now

that fucker say teach me
i wanna be a sun too

but the rice only sing in sun language
and only dances under sun people hands

we nah dance for the thief
for the harsh boots and short tempers

we don't grow for them fuckers
we don't grow in winter

and it's always always always winter in America
always Winter.

//

ants be dancin among grains of rice
it is gold, it is manna, it is blessed, it is best
consumed only by the worthy
those of thick tongue and shadow skin
those that name themselves sun-kin
the ones that find themselves in a place, sunken
the ones who need to remember again

children i am here for your lips and bellies only
i'll be a curse to the spooks that demand your bounty
i'll pass over your lands and choke the soil of your captors
and never again will i grow, not for the oppressor

you'll find me in the future, singing songs of back-home back-home
so that you'll remember who you are no matter how far we roam

thirsty

the tree i think
       is hungry
              thirsty— as fuck, perhaps

it holds itself close
       roots twisted tendrils
       knotted into fists

the ground around it cracks
       it's heartbreak
       thunderbolts of pain
       washed across the face

until: the waters

the rains are godly
and the tree, i think
has prayed for this to the sky
and has been answered
       with kissing molecules

the ground
       drinks
       in splashing great gulps

and turns its palms
       puddled with liquid glass
       to the tree

the tree
       a child — a member of the congregation
       and riddled with doubts
       searches for it

reaches

the roots' lips touch droplets
    wet manna
    cool deliverance
    life, dancing

they drink
    with need
    with desire and love and fear and
    a need
    a longing

a chronic intractable longing
    to be seen, heard
    and quenched.

a necessary violence

gnarled fingers and fine fleshy filaments fight
vie for attention
slapping and strangling and stabbing at siblings
but this is a necessary violence

survival is a gift given only to those wild enough to snatch it
and sometimes it is necessary, no? to steal
sun and water and space and time and space and time
and

we think it natural, naturally, because it happens
without thought, born only from a seed / of need

these violent creatures in their violent dance
this scrapping and scratching
does this happen, always, naturally

or is it from the seed of necessity
when the garden is overcrowded
and the resources scarce?

once

we was walking, once
upright like statues, anointed
like mountains grew legs
we was wonderful, once
song spiraling people, birds
featherless

and yet
as arrogant and as ignorant as Icarus
we sang until our voice was too hoarse to be wings
language melted from tongue like wax from feather
sold common sense for mere pennies
dressed in feathers and thick black wax
swinging among canopies
decorating forest with
windchimes and bottle trees

     we was a whole hunn'd things
     before being cast off
     god don't want us if
     we don't want us and
     i— we / can make
     purgatory smell like heaven

though the taste be foul.

the binding-binding game (Ananse)

time: binding
time: bound

bound to run outta time, no?
bound to run into time
bound to run from time

bound to run from time to time

im playing the spider game
the "binding-binding game"
the "Sky God, gimme them stories" game
dragging fairies from flamboyant trees game
and weaving leopards a prison of vines game
the hornets in the calabash game

time: binding
time: bound

how did the spider-man do it?
how do we do it now?
we allowed them to paint our god with white powder
and we bound to start believing the masquerade

time: binding
time: bound

how did Ananse do it?
spin a spiderweb up to the sky
trick the ke-keing god with cleverness and gumption
could we do it, again?
steal our stories back from this new "sky god"
who gave him the damn box anyway?

time: binding
time: bound

we bound to run outta time, no?
we bound to run into time
we bound to run from time

we bound to run from time to time

      i know i know i know
      we got nuthin but time

      but
      im thinking
      Ananse should've kept our stories
      in the box,
      locked.

      Niggas stay over-sharing
      Niggas is too kind

two blocks round Africa
for my Loves

This. This is North Philly
this is cracked sidewalks
and hip hop in neo soul
and community garden plots

What it is not
is another breeding ground for transplants and gentrifiers
though, they be here
spreading like wildfire
this is blacklands
though papi stores host other men
we roam the streets like pride of lions
everyone tryna be king
no one tryna be free

But there is a little Oasis
a little temple right in the middle
that screams black
that screams gold
that screams brass
that screams green and fertile lands
a sacred ground where spirits dance

A little bit of Africa
on Dover St
a little piece of Africa
on Dover St
spirits of the diaspora
on Dover St
visiting Africa
on Dover St

the color is:

what the wizard said
was that the color was red;
store windows burst crimson.

and if the wizard
deems the color is now green,
you bleed in chartreuse.

the wizard told you
that the new color was blue;
held your breath to be

a sickened shade of
cerulean. you would
die for the color.

what happens when your
all-powerful wizard feels
the need to transcend

red and blue, yellow
their offspring of bastard hues.
death to violet and

green, marigold and
eggplant. what, when the wizard
declares the color:

white?
what then do you give up
to be right?

bent

niggas bend over backwards
to love whiteness

they gotta have their white tees
their fresh white kicks
niggas want white money white power
white privilege white bitches

it's // orgasmic

i mean
bitches buy white baby dolls and then hand them to bawling black babies
liiiiiiike

but

like i say

niggas just lo—ve bending
over backwards
for white folks

it's // orgasmic

"bend over the ground and get my crops
bend over yo pride and feed my child
bend over that stove and cook my dinner
bend over your own busted back and do a jig for me
bend over the bleeding body of your brother and lick these boots,
nigga"

bend ova bend ova bend ova
niggas just love to bend ova

i think, maybe
it's // orgasmic

broke backs like, shiiiiiiiiiiit
heads so far up white asses

look like broken dandelions
weeds with broken stems

you know, weeds are beautiful if you know 'bout em
they resilient
as fuck
they come in and you kill 'em
and they die
then they come back, more of 'em
so, you kill 'em
and they die
but them mofos just keep coming back.

i was watching children
running across the grass
somewhere,
a whole mess of dandelions just weedy and whiteheaded
dancing, jiggin along the breeze

you know, kids, being how they be
ran clean over them shits
didn't take not one notice of em

so,
them motherfuckas got trampled
seeds thrown up in dismay like
last minute prayers

you hope (you hope you hope you hope)
that, maybe, they take root
one day

but these dandelions?
these

they dead
bleeding // broken // with stems,

bent.

we wade / we know

we wade / into
waters. washing away sense with worry
find slippery footing
amongst the muddy beds of live streams
we think:
maybe this is free?
but we don't even know what free sounds like
the rains come the beds fill and we are left
to float on greedy waves. slapping at wet claws, gasping for air
we are squeezing prayers between our teeth like oranges.

nothing compares to silence
the sound of god singing
tells us we know the words, too
but in the wee small hours of the night, we scream angrily at heaven:
      we know nothing!
      and god is too expensive right now, anyway
      now that we have spent all our freedom
      on water.

the only man who speaks it

what happens to the last black man
left 'lone with only the language of ghosts on his lips
he used to think he knew every nook + cranny of his chest
but lately it has felt less armor
more echoing + empty chamber
far from sunshine + rainbows—
somewhere, beneath his heart lies a minefield
it must be walked delicately
or perhaps, not at all
the dichotomy is sickening
empty chamber full of explosive traps
he wonders, reaching into the cavity,
this has always been here?

decay

The most ancient monuments depict the black face
The blackbody the black race

Peezy kinky curly hair
big nose big lips god eyes with black stare

The most ancient monuments depict the black face
The blackbody the black race

Olmec and Buddha
and Ramses and Moai

yes, I said it I named it we've been here since time was nothin but time
you think im lying?

tell me them ain't black face
Them lips them nose them skin them gaze

we've been here since days was just day
since all was ocean in sunrays

and now
now

The mountain people crawl to our thrones
and graciously we welcome them home
showed them our history in stone

and for reasons unknown–
No– for reasons well-known

for greed and envy and hates himself and you and me and we and hate and
we and you and hate and envy and greed and need and power and need
and power and plunder and pillage and rape

because they ain't
they wiped us away

call us anything but our names
call us anything but our names
they call us anything but our names.

white man in corner where you belong
I have no patience for your white man song
your desire to see yourself in stone
to be draped in gold to be set on the throne

but
you don't use stone

you use clay

The most ancient monuments depict the black face
The blackbody the black race

cause stone is forever
clay is decay.

pickin niggas / havin picnics

it's a true story
though gruesome how men with
pallid hands, and faces

with salivating
mouths and want-more-want-yours
bellies. hungry beasts

it is a fact that
white men indulged
in the sun-heavy

flesh of the black man
they'd be hunted and caught
and lynched and then burned

and sometimes, body
bits were sliced off and thrown
to the panting crowds:

"here: a nipple, and
here: a black cock and here:
them black balls, touch 'em

hold 'em, fondle 'em
suck 'em eat 'em, cause we
own 'em, cause we ain't

them, cause we need them
cause we want them, cause we
want to feel the sun

burning in our bowels
and bellies, filling us

like a grave, waiting"

beasts, salivating
what did they do with these
burnt black body bits?

you heard, im sure, the
story bout the word "picnic"?
what's on the menu?

they say, the taste of
nigga, it's sensual–
aphrodisiac

in st. croix, after
the hurricanes, a black
mother tells her state-

side son: baby, they
be like maggots on a
carcass you can bet

them sun-heavy grounds
taste... sensual.... maybe
taste like sun-heavy

flesh, taste of blackness
taste like blackness taste like
niggas. niggas. nig –

we / sun people / mypeople

people
my
people

cookout
people
bonfire
people
summer
people

fucking

sun
people
love
people
XmasPartyLateAsShitYouAintGotsToGoHomeButDamn
people

my
people
mine
people.

when / we were

when we were then
when we were there

when we were present

when we were laughter plastered across the sky
when we were travelers, so far gone, so high
when we were dancers along foreign shores
when we were children pretending to be dinosaurs

when we were swimming among stars, in a soup of turquoise gems
when we were eating sweet fruits, caressing cheeks, kissing hands
when we were rum drunk and then sun drunk and drunk on love
when we were made small, awed by the sight of mountains reaching from
above

when we were a galaxy, skin bespeckled with tiny prisms
when we were a world without war, no chasms, no schisms
when we were a school of fish, playing amorous among coral
when we were smiling farmlands, teeming with life and rich black soil

when we was wandering
when we was there and then and present

when we were golder, bolder
we were light, we were contented.

you aint been —

you aint been home in a minute

aint been here to lie on lush carpet
aint turned your nose into the threads to inhale the sultry smell of casso-
lette

you aint been here to nuzzle deep
into pillows, to wrap crushing arms around the spine of your bed

you aint even been home to pop into the kitchen
tryna peep my secrets, running fingers light 'cross surfaces

home, it's like a ghost town
haunted by the echoes of your staff, your fingertips, your tongue, your lips

we fight / dirty

clashin'
the sound of words
smackin' each other 'cross
the mouth / you call her bitch
she call you her father and he
been gone.

syrup / honey

commitment pours thick, syrup
thick, honey

does honey go rancid
does it transition well, sweet to not

wadnt ready to jump
but jump we did

commitment never sweet, not water
never easy flow, not water

it is thick, paint
jelly

something changeable
something molded

something solid
heavy + thick

sticky.

a virus

We are the virus
Contaminating all containers
And still we beg to be held

Sometimes I debate my own aliveness to myself
We arent here we are here we aint here we aint nothin
And yet I dream and make earthside plans

We are so contagious
A body of decay and desperation
Misery loves company, we love a party

We break bodies across boundaries
And leave horrendous counts of corpses
All the arms we ran into, wanting

We are the virus
And we just want to be home
We just cant find a home

My man can only be host
As I am not living, not here we aint here
And I — ravage him

Digging into the soft parts of him
Looking to be let in, looking for warmth
Burrowing, breaking across membranes

When I wrap my arms around him
He feels it like cold fingers, a force around his throat
He wheezes away from me in tears

He runs from me in fear
I was just trying to be at home

I was just tryna be here
We are the virus
We here
But we really aint here.

the quarantine poems

i.
it's a nightmarish sight
the sky has bled black into the parking lot
and three stories up feels more like seven
im, slightly, tempted by the sea that
sky and cement had begrudgingly birthed
outside my window
the ground shrugs in a wave of spirit hands
"you stay you stay you stay" they whine
"come here come here come here" some hiss
voices so seductive, so sly, so sumptuous, i almost oblige.

ii.
metal slugs leave steaming tracks of slime
like they always do, but now it seems… slower
birds the size of house flies beg to be squashed
against the powder blue walls of this cage
noses pressed with greed and need against glass
the beasts are getting restless
the air teases and tempts with taunts that it can carry you
where? away from here? where do we run?
i used to dream of flying— jumping smoothly out my window to soar
now i realize even lost boys probably just want to come home.

iii.
the children // are begging for my attention
but i don't know that i have it in me to give.

the wild geese from outside are calling and i curse them
shut the fuck up. i cannot answer the call today.

today i will be resolute in my lonely
stand fully— righteously alone ….

i wish for the numbers that will grant me leave of this place

flight— i would answer the call for flight,

sometimes the geese are silent, floating upon mirrors and smoke
resolute in their quiet, maybe not lonely // maybe at peace.

spice + orange

spice +
orange +
sometimes popcorn
+ tea
+ stories
+ Babyface
live, MTV
+ naps
in the
sun, in
midday on
the couch
so green
we be
riding on
fields blooming
with sleep
+ yawns
+ pillars
like flowers.

violent

i feel
i am on fire

i feel aflame with red
i need to pull this burning skin off
pound the pain out of my head

a bitch is seeing red
a bitch is burning red
a bitch is wishing for an end
a bitch is waiting to be dead

i wanna fee— l
violet
because i bur— n
violent
and im not in-
violate
and i ca— n't
fight it

i wanna take— flight
and if i don't make it

perhaps
that's all right

spiritgirl, guilty

the dead-gone folks say
you act like you don't want to stay

guilty as charged– i've had to be coaxed into my body
any attempts to claim it as home have been nothing short of shoddy

if it's a temple then I tell you for many years, god weren't present
just a few wizened ghosts, some beggars, some peasants

the tithe box is empty
the altar be dusty

the stained glass been spiderweb-cracked
the air is thick with neglect, fat

the dead-gone folks say
little spirit, you can stay you can stay

guilty as charged– i make pilgrimage back to the body
living is religion, it is expected, it is godly

the body

he heard that heaven
is in between her thighs
but then
is that where *god* resides?

don't *god* got a whole temple
a whole palace, a whole body
to reside in?
to thrive in?

do *god* only lounge in the
velvet and silk of the womb and
labia and liquids souped with
primordial spores?

do *god* only swim in them seas
don't *god* sometimes reside in the belfry
glancing resigned down 'pon the rest of the body
the kingdom, the country

don't *god* got a good view from up there?

the weight of

the turtle— do you think
he feels the burden of house arrest
carrying the weight of home–
is it all that arresting?

i think i've carried home with me
for so long, i count its weight as my own
i can't calculate my own age
without counting the swirls and cracks upon my back

for the turtle home is visible
we think it a box one is cuffed to for life
but perhaps it is less of a house and more
of the being itself

who's to say the weight of home
is arresting to one
who carries it as part of body, as part of self
everyday.

mother / nature

with that mouth
you kiss your mother
violence is of course
well within our nature
we battle, deal deadly blows
famine, genocide, missile strikes
with that mouth, foul, you pray
your mother kisses you   back.

receive the sacrament

your mouth is open
your hands are open
your heart is open
your mind–
is praying to gods
please, heal me

you need me
i can be your god
i can be placed like his flesh on your tongue

swallow me
 gulp down your last hope
 when you've run out of sense
 and all that's left is desire
 feel me
                – dissolve
                like pixie dust sprinkled
                along bloodstream
                you feel me
                release
an evil begged for, unleashed.

"we should make a list"

it was said
that maybe   we should make a list
                        of all the times we prayed
                        into the oceanic silence of cupped hands
if we did
then maybe   we'd interpret
                        wind songs as psalms
                        maybe when we wail into our palms
and hold them
conch-like
to panting ears
                        we'd notice
                        that silence
                        is an answer.

weeping

lying in the shadow
of the blessed branches
of a weeping cherry tree

we catch butterflies
and caterpillars
get examined and tickled by ladybugs

things were simpler then
we saw weeping and thought Grand Mother
and felt ourselves be loved by the earth

and today midst the
burglary and bane
we find weeping to mean sorrow

and we lay dumbstruck and supine
let the tears run down our back
moaning how far heaven looks from here

and the poem could end there
'cept i still see weeping and think Grand Mother
playing at youth among insects, still so loved.

ifa turns my tears to joy
for Gabrielle

Ifasoekunmidayo
my tears, my tears, my tears

they were monsoons upon my face
now i turn, i turn, i turn

my palms
in submission to the Ori.

my godmother
is a library

and i
am an eager deity

Ifasoekunmidayo
i am draped in beads of Oshun

the ageless
god with many names

i can patiently wait
for her answer to my call: Omitorera.

we are but ancients
dusted in white, rooted in here

Ifasoekunmidayo
my tears, my tears, my tears

have been turned
to pearls of joy

i place them
on the altar

i pray
only to me.

the streets will mourn before you will

sidewalk— begin keening, wailing into dolent nights
fire hydrants— bawl openly in the streets
powerlines— wrap arms around grieving homes
sneakers— dangle like keepsake charms of ghosts

the sun sits and sets
on a block riddled with misery and rue
doesn't rise with the same vigor, ever again

is that the tipping point
when the very sky cracks open at its joints
to mourn your child, gone

will that then shake you 'wake?

streets stuck in a gasp, midcry
blacktop— the real blackness that mothered your baby
broke and purposeless.

earth raises fists   and shakes the ground in protest.
clouds will   fall around your ears
waters flooding the streets, wiping away echoes
of young laughter.

we will all be ghosts —
              the block, an abandoned wartime ruin —
before you, yourself
raise fists to the boogeyman
who devour our children?

circuses (04 july)

i don't know what we would have called it
had we not known a name
from the hook of Geb's elbow
it sprouted
but it was from the empyrean
that it rained

what. did. i. know. of science and mechanics
explosives and combustion
i knew only periwinkle stars winking coquettishly
at fuchsia blooms
i. stared. as. magic was belched from the ground and bubbled against black
oceans i knew smoke, a noxious cloud
floating up — stream through the void
i knew the sound of thunder kissing a whip-crack
of echoing dirty hands slamming together in amazement

mirrored, it was, in my own glassy eyes
as i stood birds nest high
and watched the sky
raining fire

the color of flowers and smiles
what. did. i. know. of power and might
omniscience and ownership
i knew the audacity of throwing so much flame
into the heaving bosom of Nut
and i wonder now
if she bears smokers' lung as result
i know that what is cause for celebration is often a lie
but it can be made to taste sweet
i know the spectacle of a night lit with birthday candles
blown out before we could question their motive

lit // like a slap against the ironic black
i know now
the circuses we've been audience to
the beating and whipping of our gods

we watch the skies
reign fire, daily   i don't know what to call it

                              other than its name.

Born and raised in Philadelphia, Khaliah D. Pitts is a writer, multidisciplinary artist and speaker dedicated to crafting spaces of liberation, celebration and joy. Her artistic practice is storytelling as a means of cultural and self- preservation. She explores in the mediums of literature, video art, memory/altarwork, land and kitchen and land based arts. Khaliah considers herself a cultural memory-worker, documenting stories of the African diaspora, crafting spaces of liberation and joy.